The Big Sniff

The Biggest Sniff in the Whole History of the World 2

The Witch of Withy Bottom 10

The Reverend Frogmorton 16

Trapped 20

The Secrets of Withy Bottom 26

The Fat Bishop 34

Abby and the Armada 38

The Battle of Withy Bottom 44

The End of the Witch of Withy Bottom 50

The Mystery of Woodford Green 60

Written by Eric Johns

Illustrated by Zara Slattery

Collins Educational

An imprint of HarperCollins*Publishers*

1

The Biggest Sniff in the Whole History of the World

Abby was worried. Something strange was happening to her, but she didn't know what.

She sniffed.

A boy came running towards her waving his arms. His face was screwed up in fright and his mouth was open as if he was yelling – but there was no sound.

Abby jumped out of the way in alarm. But the boy vanished like her breath on a cold morning.

In front of her, Abby saw her nan marching smartly towards the park gates at the end of the road. She blinked several times to make sure what she was seeing was really there. Everything seemed normal.

"Keep up," Nan called.

Abby ran a few paces.

Every afternoon, Nan met her at the school gates and took her to stay at her house until her mum came to collect her. But before that, Nan took her on a walking race to have some fresh air. She was mad about fresh air. Abby wanted to go straight home to watch television, and she said so every day. But Nan didn't approve of television.

It was on these walking races that Abby began to smell pictures.

"Breathe deeply," Nan called over her shoulder.

Abby sniffed cautiously.

"Don't sniff," Nan said sharply. "Use your hanky."

"I wasn't sniffing," Abby replied. "I was smelling."

Nan said "Tut-tut," which meant that she thought the kindest thing to do was to ignore what Abby just said.

Abby's nose twitched. Ghostly horses appeared in front of her.

"Oh, no," she groaned.

"What did you say?" Nan asked.

"There used to be horses here," Abby announced.

Nan stopped suddenly and Abby nearly crashed into her.

They peered up the driveway of a big house.

"That's right," Nan said. "There were no cars when this house was built, and the garage was once a stable." She patted Abby on the head. "I'm pleased to see you keeping your eyes open."

"No," Abby tried to explain. "I meant I could smell horses."

"Silly girl." Nan gave a small frown. "There haven't been horses here for eighty years or more." She trotted off again. "Come along now. Don't dawdle."

Abby sighed and hurried after Nan's clacking shoes. It was no use trying to explain. She knew it wouldn't be. But she could smell horses – that was what was wrong.

Every time she took one of the deep breaths Nan was so keen on, she smelt things that weren't there any more and pictures jumped into her head. Like the horses she'd just seen.

When she had first started smelling pictures, they'd been fuzzy, like looking in a steamed up mirror. But slowly they had been getting clearer. It was as if her nose was learning how to make pictures in more detail.

Then suddenly today, the pictures weren't in her head any more. They were like cars coming towards her on a foggy day. One second they weren't there, then they leapt at her as solid as everything else in the street. None of the things she'd sniffed before had been as real as the frightened boy or the horses.

It was all a bit scary. She hurried after her nan, trying to take tiny breaths. She had a feeling that a big sniff might be dangerous.

"Can't we go home and watch television?" Abby pleaded. "Everyone else does."

"Breathe deeply," Nan shouted, as usual taking no notice of any mention of television. "What you need is some fresh sea air. Sitting in a stuffy classroom all day is no good for a growing girl."

Nan sped away and Abby pursued her. They went through the park where the ducks swam on the pond and along the path by the river to the place where it flowed into the sea. There they paused to look across the bay at the oil rig which was Nan's worst enemy.

"Ugly monster!" she cried, as if casting a spell to make it float out to sea and disappear.

Abby looked up at her Nan. She wore an old hat with a long drooping feather in it and shoes that snapped at the pavement. She wasn't like her friend's grandmothers. Even Mr Alfreds, Abby's class teacher, had noticed her.

As soon as she remembered Mr Alfreds, Abby felt angry again, just as she had at school that afternoon. When they were getting ready to go home, Mr Alfreds had said, "Well, Abigail Angel, who's the lady that comes to collect you every day?"

This made Abby angry for two reasons. One was that she could tell he thought her Nan was funny, and the other was that he made fun of her name. He said her first name in full, and used her surname more often than anyone else's in the class. Abigail Angel. He was always saying it and laughing at her.

Nan had told her that they'd got their name from a foreign sailor who'd been shipwrecked in the bay and never gone home again. He'd got married and there'd been a family called Angel in the town ever since. Because he'd come from another country, their family had black hair and dark eyes.

Abby didn't like Mr Alfreds because he made her feel different. And he was always picking on her friend Walid as well.

"A real character, your nan," Mr Alfreds had said to Abby, smiling as if he expected her to be on his side and laugh at Nan. "Is it her you take after I wonder?"

"I'd rather take after Nan," Abby had said to Walid, "than look like Mr Alfreds."

"He looks like a clown," Walid had said.

"With a red face and a yellow wig," Abby added, and then they'd laughed secretly.

If Walid hadn't been in her class, she'd have been very lonely.

Nan interrupted her daydreaming. "Come on. No sniffing. Breathe in – one, two, three."

The feather in her hat quivered blackly against the sky and her nose was like the beak of a hawk about to swoop.

They turned their backs on the oil rig and hurried round a corner by a pub called The Angel Inn. There was a sign showing an angel holding a tankard of beer.

"Why's this pub called the Angel Inn?" Abby asked, hoping that talking about something else might make her stop thinking about smelling pictures. "What's an angel got to do with beer? Is that the angel we're named after?"

"Silly girl." Nan stopped again and Abby skidded to a halt. "The first Mr Angel in Woodford Green was a sailor not an airman." She looked at the pub sign. "I expect something happened in the past which made people give it that name," she suggested. "Now breathe in, fill your lungs."

Abby breathed shallowly, but even so her nose tingled. She knew she was going to see something but had no idea what. Her smells were rather vague so the scent of cut-grass might bring a picture of a lawn mower, or a picnic, or a battle in a field.

Suddenly, two men on horseback came charging towards her, their legs flapping in panic. She flung her arms up to protect herself. The men dissolved as they were about to ride over her.

She had no sooner lowered her arms than she found herself surrounded by men in armour. Just as quickly they vanished.

"That's better," Nan cried happily.

"There was a battle here once," Abby told her.

"Nonsense," Nan said briskly. "No-one would be allowed to have a battle in Woodford Green."

"There was. I just smelt it."

Nan gave her a look and raised one eyebrow.

"That's enough of that silliness." She turned quickly to stop Abby continuing. "One good, deep breath and we'll go straight home for tea. I don't think we'll bother with the rest of our walk today."

"Can I watch television?" Abby asked.

"Just this once," Nan promised.

Abby was delighted. Nan had never given in before.

She was so pleased about getting out of the walking race that she forgot about smelling pictures. She did as she was told and took a deep breath. In through her nose, mouth closed, as Nan always told her.

In – counting – one, two, three, four, five. Then she was supposed to blow all the breath out in one. But there was no out. The sniff went on and on. It was the biggest sniff she had ever taken.

Six, seven, eight, nine, ten.

Whirling pictures of strange people filled her head.

Eleven, twelve, thirteen, fourteen, fifteen.

Her nose seemed to have decided to do what it liked.

"Stop!" she tried to yell at it.

But her nose sniffed on.

It was like a dog let off its lead for a run. It searched everywhere for smells. It welcomed every single one into its twitching nostrils. It wanted more and more smells – bigger, wilder, more mysterious, never-smelled before smells.

"Help!" Abby tried to shout. "I'm going dizzy."

Sixteen, seventeen, eighteen, nineteen, twenty. Pictures of strange-looking people spun round her.

She closed her eyes. They were still there.

"Whatever is the matter?" she heard her Nan ask, but her voice seemed a long way away.

Her legs went wobbly, like the time she'd stayed on the roundabout in the park too long.

There was a thump as Abby hit the ground.

"Ouf!" she exploded. All the breath she had sniffed seemed to go out of her in one woosh!

Her head was still spinning, but she felt quite proud of her nose. It had broken the world's biggest record for sniffs.

"That was the biggest sniff in the whole history of the world," she gasped.

She waited with her eyes closed for Nan to tell her that it was rude to sniff. But there was no sound. No tut-tut.

The world stopped going round.

Abby opened her eyes and looked up.

There was a circle of strange faces looking down at her.

2

The Witch of Withy Bottom

"Who are you?" Abby demanded in alarm, looking at the circle of the unknown faces bending over her.

"We know who we are," a man with a scabby head and dirty hair told her. "The question is, who be you?"

"Her's a witch!" a red-faced boy with yellowish hair announced. He looked about fifteen and rather mean, Abby thought. There was something familiar about him.

"Shut yer yap, Alf," an old woman snapped at him. "You can see her's only a child."

"I saw her fall off her broomstick," Alf told the others. Several of them nodded.

"Broomstick!" Abby cried, struggling to her feet a bit shakily. "Fiddlesticks! Where is it, then?" Abby demanded fiercely. "Tell me that, Alf!"

"How do her know my name, if her bain't a witch?" Alf asked.

"I just said it, you girt lummock," the old woman said, and slapped him round the head before he could duck.

"Nan!" Abby suddenly cried, looking around.

"Yes, dear?" the old woman replied.

"How do her know your name then?" Alf asked, putting out his tongue in triumph. "'Tis plain. Her's a witch."

"What have you done with my nan?" Abby asked, taking a step towards Alf. He jumped back. "I en't done nothing," he squealed.

"Have you lorst your nan?" the old woman asked, smiling kindly with black and yellow teeth.

"She was here with me. Then I took this huge sniff and… " Abby looked round her. "Where am I?" she cried.

"Why, dear, you're in the parish of Withy Bottom."

Abby looked at the houses on each side of the road. They were like the old-fashioned black and white ones that she and Nan passed on their walking races. Only, the wooden parts were not shiny black, but were the colour of wood that had been left out in the rain; and the wall parts were not white, but looked like dried mud with stones in it; and the thatch was not neatly trimmed, but more like hair which was going bald and hadn't been brushed for a week; and the road was a muddy track.

Abby turned back to the people. They were dirty and ragged and their clothes looked funny. Suddenly she realised why.

"*When* am I?" she wailed.

"What do her mean?" Alf demanded.

"What's the date?" Abby cried. "What year is it?"

The circle of faces frowned.

"I do believe it be 1588," the old man said, scratching a scab on his head.

"Ooooh!" Abby gave a long drawn out cry. "I want to go home."

"There, there, dear," Alf's nan said, putting her arm round Abby and crushing her face comfortingly in the folds of her ragged skirt. "What lovely hair you do have," she said, stroking Abby's dark curls.

Abby gave one sob, then held her breath. If she took another noseful while she was buried in Nan's clothes, she would faint. Nan might be kind but she smelt as though she hadn't washed for a year or two.

Abby pushed herself free of Nan's hugging and stared defiantly at the circle of faces. They were watching her the way cows do when a stranger walks through their field.

The man with the scabby head looked at her hard and suddenly his face lit up. "Her be lorst," he exclaimed, nodding happily at having had such a brilliant idea. "That's it. Her be lorst."

"Oh, well done," Abby snorted at him.

"Of course her be lorst," Nan snapped. "If you didn't have a turnip for a head, you'd have seed that five minutes since."

"Where d'you live then?" Alf wanted to know.

"I come from Woodford Green," Abby told them, "and I should be grateful if you would help me get back there."

"Never heard of it," Alf said, as if that proved

Abby was lying. "I bet there's no such place. I say her's a witch." About half the heads nodded.

It was at that moment that Abby made a decision. Alf was over four hundred years behind her, and she wasn't going to be called a witch by the likes of him. She'd done enough history to know that witches used to end up on a ducking-stool taking a bath in the village pond. So while she was here she wasn't going to be called a witch.

What she would be, she decided after taking a closer look at the circle of faces, was the boss of this village. Most of the people looked as if they'd be happy to be told what to do.

"If I were a witch, Alf," she told him, screwing up her face and staring hard, "you'd be hopping about in the pond by now going 'croak, croak, croak'."

Alf, underneath the dirt which covered most of his face, turned paler.

Suddenly Abby remembered why he looked familiar. He was the frightened boy she'd seen running towards her after one of her sniffs.

Abby took a deep breath. "Right, everyone listen. My name is Abby Angel."

"More like the Devil Angel," Alf muttered.

"While I am here, I shall stay with Alf's Nan, if she will let me."

"Of course you shall, me dear," Nan smiled.

"Next," Abby went on, "I shall need someone to show me around." No-one jumped to offer. "You." She pointed at a dark-haired boy who had been watching her carefully but had not said anything. He seemed to be about the same age as her. "What's your name?"

"Walter," the boy said suspiciously.

"I shall call you Wally." He looked a bit more alert than some of the others, Abby thought.

Now she was ready to explore the place and see if she could find some way back to Woodford Green and her own time. She didn't want a crowd following her, especially not Alf, but how could she get rid of them?

That's easy, she told herself. I'm the boss, so I'll just tell them.

"Wally, you'll come with me. The rest of you can go on with your work." She dismissed them with a wave.

As the crowd parted, she saw the dark figure of a man hurrying up the muddy street towards them. Alf saw him too and his face split into a cunning grin.

3

THE REVEREND FROGMORTON

Alf ran towards the figure stumbling up the street.

"Come quick," he yelled excitedly. "We've caught a witch. Her fell off a broomstick."

"Who's that?" Abby asked.

"The Reverend Frogmorton," Wally replied. "He's the priest for our village. You'd best be careful."

Wally seemed to have decided that if Alf was against her she couldn't be all that bad.

"Thanks for the warning, Wally."

The Reverend Frogmorton panted up to her. He was skinny and leathery like a beetle, and wore thick black tights under his cloak. His clothes weren't so ragged as everyone else's.

The crowd closed around her again.

"Now then, who are you?" he blew bad breath all over her. "Answer truly or I shall know. I am a learned man."

"Well," Abby said, "if you're that clever, you'll know that Alf's a fool and you won't pay any attention to him."

"I don't need to be told what to think by an ignorant child."

"Who are you calling ignorant?" Abby demanded. "I go to school. I bet I know more than you."

"Her's lying," Alf cried, giving a little dance. "Girls don't go to school."

"I warn you child," the Reverend Frogmorton said, showing a row of black teeth in what was supposed to be a threatening scowl but which Abby thought made him look rather foolish. "The truth or it will be the worse for you."

"Everyone goes to school where I come from, it doesn't matter whether you're a boy or girl."

"Her's lying, her's lying," Alf chanted. "Witches allus lie."

"Do you say that you can read, girl?" The Reverend Frogmorton asked, curling his lip disbelievingly.

"I've been able to read since I was five," Abby said indignantly.

The Reverend Frogmorton dug in a leather pouch hanging from his belt. He pulled out a piece of thick yellow paper and jabbed it at her.

"Read this, and if you can't I shall have you whipped."

Abby unfolded the paper. It was covered in strange, black letters. "What language is this?"

"Latin, girl, what else would it be?"

"I don't speak Latin do I, I'm English, so I learned to read English. And I've just started French," Abby added.

"French!" Alf exclaimed. "Her's a Spaniard! Her's a spy!"

"Spaniards speak Spanish," Abby told him scornfully. "French speak French."

"Her's a Spaniard," Alf insisted. "Her's a spy *and* a witch."

"Be silent, Alf," the Reverend Frogmorton ordered.

"I'll write you something," Abby offered. She wriggled a pencil stub out of the pocket of her jeans and wrote on the back of the paper.

The Reverend Frogmorton read slowly, like someone just learning, "Alf – is – a – fool."

"That's the first sensible thing you've said," Abby told him, giggling. "Now do you believe girls go to school where I come from?"

The Reverend Frogmorton twitched his nose at her. "If you are a girl," he said.

The circle of faces surrounding her suddenly seemed to notice her jeans for the first time.

"Girls don't wear breeches," Alf cried out.

"I shall examine the child," the Reverend Frogmorton announced.

"What do you mean?" Abby asked suspiciously.

"To prove whether or not you be a girl-child."

"You're not examining me," Abby declared. "We saw a video at school about men like you."

"Video? I know not what you say."

"Her's mad," Alf piped up again. He seemed pleased with this new idea. "Her's mad," he repeated. "Her's mad *and* a spy *and* a witch."

"I don't have time to stand here disputing. Come with me, child." The Reverend Frogmorton stretched out a bony claw to her.

"If you touch me," Abby warned him, "I'll kick and I'll scratch and I'll bite. And my teeth are sharp – not like your rotten stumps." She bared her teeth in a ferocious snarl.

The Reverend Frogmorton snatched his hand back as if he had already been bitten.

"Perhaps the child is mad."

"Her's not mad," Nan spoke out suddenly. "Her's just frightened as anyone would be who's lorst."

"Do you care for her?" the Reverend Frogmorton asked, seeing a way out of an awkward situation.

"Her's staying with me," Nan told him.

"Then I leave her in your keeping until the Lord Bishop comes this afternoon. He shall decide what sort of creature it is."

Abby snorted at being called 'it'.

The Reverend Frogmorton turned to the circle of villagers. "Why are you standing there like idle sheep? You have work to do and the Lord Bishop comes for his rents. We'll see plenty of energy then – all going into excuses about why you're too poor to pay."

The villagers shuffled away and the Reverend Frogmorton hurried off down the the muddy street like a bandy-legged beetle.

"This afternoon," he shouted over his shoulder, "the Lord Bishop will decide."

Abby was left with Wally.

4

TRAPPED

Abby looked at Wally. He seemed to have decided that he liked her.

"You bain't really a witch, is you?" he asked.

"What do you think?"

"I think you just be ordinary but different."

"That's about it," Abby agreed.

"You give old Frogface what for," Wally laughed. "I enjoyed that. He beat me once for missing church and going fishing. Hey," he hopped two paces, having a sudden idea. "Would you like me to show you summin secret?"

"Yes. I want to see everything. I've got to find a way home to Woodford Green." Abby's voice fell and she wiped away a surprise tear. Now that the crowd had gone she was beginning to feel how completely lost she was. Not just in a strange place but in history as well.

"Where be Woodford Green?" Wally asked. "I've never heard of anywhere round here by that name."

"I don't know," Abby sighed. "Somewhere in the future, I think."

They walked up the muddy street. Abby studied each house carefully.

"I can't fathom what you say," Wally told her.

"I don't understand it myself," Abby admitted. "I did this big sniff and could smell all these things that weren't there anymore, and somehow I sniffed my way back into the past. More than four hundred years, I think."

"That be the strangest thing I've ever heard." Wally did not seem to doubt that what she said was true.

"I'm going to try something." Abby tugged her handkerchief out of her pocket. "Ready?" She blew hard. Nothing happened. "I thought I might do a sniff in reverse and blow myself back to the future."

"You must be rich," Wally said.

"Why's that?"

"T'have a kerchief. Me, I just uses me fingers." He blew his nose through his fingers to show her and wiped them in some grass.

Abby made a disgusted noise.

Suddenly she caught hold of his arm. "Who lives there?" She pointed at a house that was as old and dilapidated as all the others but that she felt sure she knew.

"That be where Alf's Nan lives."

"It's the same one," Abby whispered thoughtfully. "If you patched up the thatch and painted it and put in double glazing instead of those shutters and rags, it would be my Nan's house. You'd need to build on a garage at the side as well."

Wally was frowning.

"Don't you see what this means?" she asked. "I'm still in Woodford Green."

"Well, I doesn't see how that helps," Wally said.

"Neither do I. But at least I'm only lost in history now. It makes me feel a bit better."

"I suppose it would," Wally said looking doubtful.

"Withy Bottom isn't a very rich village, is it?" Abby remarked.

Wally shook his head. "We had two oxen once, but they got sick and died. Everyone said it were witchcraft. Since then we can't plough properly so we doesn't grow as much."

"Why don't you buy more oxen?"

"No money," Wally said glumly. "What we have got goes to the Bishop for rents."

"What's that building?" Abby pointed to a large stone building some way off.

"That be the mill. Come on, I'll race you there."

They ran past the last of the houses that made the one street of the village and along an even narrower track. There'll be a park and a duck pond here one day, Abby thought.

"Oh, it's a water mill," she exclaimed, as they squelched up to the bank which surrounded the mill pond.

"What else 'ud it be?" Wally asked.

"I thought of a windmill at first."

"I en't heard of one of them," he admitted.

"It's a funny place, the past," Abby said. "Though I don't suppose it is to you."

"Tain't to me," Wally agreed. "See that." He nodded towards a stretch of marshy ground where what looked like reeds were growing. "Those be our withy beds. The village is called Withy Bottom because of them."

"What are they for?"

"We make lobster pots from withy sticks."

Abby looked round. "The river's just over there," she pointed, "and the sea is that way."

"How do you know?"

"I live here. Or I shall do one day."

Wally nodded sadly as though he understood.

"Withy Bottom were an island before the mill pond were made. We still get cut off from the mainland if there be a lot of rain or if Master Ned the miller opens the sluice-gate and floods they marshes."

They stood for a while watching the mill wheel creak slowly round. Water trickled between the edges of the sluice-gate and the wall.

Abby noticed a muddy track that ran through the reeds. It seemed to be the way out of Withy Bottom.

Suddenly all she wanted to do was get away from the strangeness. Before she knew what she was going to do, she started running. She sprinted along the muddy track. If she ran fast enough she would leave behind the feeling of being lost and alone.

Wally gave a cry. "Come back!"

He started after her.

"Wait. Tain't no use. You've got to meet the Bishop and his Clerk."

Abby didn't run far. She soon slowed to a trot and halted. The withy sticks towered above her head. If she met anyone she'd have to stop or go blundering into the marsh. She knew that running wasn't the way to escape. Not that she knew what was. She was trapped. She'd no choice but to wait and see what happened.

She sniffed. "Sorry, Wally. I wasn't trying to get away from you."

"S'all right," Wally said. "I know how you feels."

He snapped off a reed and began to peel it. "D'you want to see a secret?" he asked. "You've got to promise not to tell, mind."

"I've never told a secret in my life," Abby said proudly, blinking a few times.

"C'mon then, I'll show you two secrets."

He's trying to make me forget about being trapped here, Abby thought.

5

The Secrets of Withy Bottom

Wally led Abby past the mill pond and along the river bank to a fallen willow tree. He climbed along the trunk, leaned over the water and tugged at something hidden under the branches.

Slowly, like a majestic liner leaving port, a raft floated into view.

"A raft," Abby exclaimed. "That's wonderful."

"'Tis a boat not a raft," Wally corrected her.

"Boats have sides. That's flat."

"'Tis a flat boat just now because I haven't build the sides yet."

"Did you make it yourself?"

He steered the boat alongside the tree. "No-one else knows about it."

"Thanks for showing me." She gave him a specially grateful smile.

Wally blushed.

"Can we go on the river?"

He nodded. "But don't tell nobody. I en't supposed to go on the river alone."

"You won't be alone. I'll be with you."

"That's all right then, isn't it?"

They laughed at their cleverness and pushed off.

The raft floated easily. There were two paddles which were made from a branch split in half. At first the current spun them in circles. They found that the best way to paddle was with one kneeling at the front paddling to the left and the other at the back paddling to the right.

"This be much better than on my own," Wally exclaimed.

"I thought you weren't allowed to go alone?"

"That be another secret," Wally laughed.

After paddling for a few minutes, the rough logs began to cut into their knees. "We'll put rushes to kneel on next time," Wally promised as they headed back to shore.

Will I be here long enough for a next time? Abby wondered.

When the raft was hidden once more, they walked on along the river bank. After a few minutes they came to a thick black pool of liquid which lay a few paces from the water's edge.

"What is it?" Abby asked.

"'Tis the Devil's Punch Bowl," Wally told her, which didn't explain much.

Abby broke off a thick reed and stuck it in the liquid. When she lifted it out, thick black strands dripped slowly off it like treacle.

"It's like oil," she said, watching it. "Does it burn?"

"It did once," Wally frowned, remembering. "It were struck by lightning and burned for a month until the spring tides came up the river and drowned the flames. No-one comes near it now because they say it's evil."

"Except for you, Wally."

"Well, that's different."

"I know. You're ordinary but different."

Wally ducked his head smiling.

"One day," Abby said, waving her arm in the direction of the river mouth and sea, "an oil rig will stand out there and pump oil to the shore. I bet this is something to do with the lot under the sea."

"Can't see much use for it."

"Well," Abby tried to think how to explain it. No use saying cars needed oil. Wally wouldn't know a car from a camera. "You can use oil to light your house at night or cook your food."

"I see," Wally said, but he didn't sound very interested. "I'll show you summin else. My other secret." By the excitement in his voice, Abby guessed he thought this was far more interesting.

Just above the black pool of the Devil's Punch Bowl the river bank became steeper. Wally climbed up a little way and scratched a hole in the sand. A tiny cave appeared. Abby squinted to see inside. Some funny, lumpy shapes became visible in the gloom.

"What are they?"

Wally reached inside and pulled one out.

"Pots," he said.

Abby put her head on one side. "I've never seen any that shape before."

"Nor had anyone else, till Alf made them,"

Wally laughed. "I'll tell you the tale. Alf works for Tom the potter. There be a good seam of clay the other side of the village and Tom's pots sell well."

Abby nodded, wondering what was coming.

"So one day Tom left Alf to make they easy pots himself. But Alf be too lazy to do a good job, unless Tom beats him everyday, so he put too much wet with the clay and tried to bake them quickly before they sagged."

"He didn't succeed, did he?" Abby said, examining the wonky clay pot.

"There be more to this yet," Wally grinned. "When Tom Potter saw the mess Alf had made of such a simple job, he said he'd beat Alf black and blue if he didn't make up the money he'd lost him. Well, Alf puts the pots in a basket on the cart and says he be a-goin' to market to sell them. No-one believed he would. But he were back the next morning saying he'd sold them to a merchant. Alf were very pleased with himself. He told a fine story about fooling the merchant into thinking that the pots were the latest shape from France. He jingled his purse while he talked and in the end paid Tom what he owed him."

"So what are the pots doing here?" Abby asked, looking at Wally suspiciously.

"That be a good question." Wally looked very pleased with himself. "But an even better one is, if Alf lied about selling them pots, where did he get the money?"

"I know your sort, Wally," Abby said. "You don't ask a question like that unless you've already got the answer."

"Well, I do think I have." He grinned. "I had to go to town the day after Alf sold the pots, and everyone were gossiping about how someone had stolen the Poor Box from the Bishop's own church. There were a fair bit of money in it according to the tale."

"Doesn't anyone else know about this?"

Wally shook his head. "No-one knows about the pots except me – and Alf, of course. The next time anyone from Withy Bottom went to market, something else were news and the thieving were forgotten."

"You're a sly one, Wally," Abby said, sucking in her cheeks. "Why haven't you said anything about it?"

"I thought it might be useful to have summin against Alf one day. He be a bully and not one to have for an enemy, and him and me don't get on."

They put the pots back and filled up the hole in the bank. Wally looked at the sky and said it was time to get back for the Bishop's visit. They went on down the path by the river until they came to the sand dunes. There were some fishing boats on the beach and they saw Alf sitting on one gazing out across the bay.

"He be on watch," Wally said.

"Watching for what?" Abby asked.

"The Spanish fleet. All the fishing villages have been told to keep a lookout," Wally explained. "We has to light a beacon if any ships are sighted."

"We learned about the Spanish ships in history," Abby told him.

"Anyways," Wally went on, "it be all because King Philip of Spain wants to be king of England as well. But we ain't having that."

"Who's 'we'?" Abby asked, laughing. "You and Queen Elizabeth?"

Wally gave her a shove. "Come on," he shouted, starting to run. "We'll be late for the Bishop."

They panted to the top of the sand dunes and slid down the other side. Abby found herself back in the village street.

The first thing she saw were two horses with saddles, harnesses and cloths on them.

"The Bishop and his Clerk be here," Wally whispered, more from sudden nervousness than because there was anyone near enough to hear.

Alf's nan came hurrying down the street towards them.

"Quickly now," she puffed. "The good Bishop wants to see you. Answer politely and call him *my Lord*."

The horses were tethered outside the biggest

house in the village and all the villagers seemed to be surrounding it.

"That be The Ship Inn," Wally said, whispering again.

That's where The Angel Inn will be one day, Abby thought.

At that moment, the Reverend Frogmorton came scuttling out. He peered up and down the street, saw Abby and snapped his fingers at her.

"Quick girl, or whatever you are," he screeched. "The Lord Bishop doesn't like to be kept waiting."

Abby patted one of the horses as she went by. It nodded its head at her and made the cloth on its reins flap.

"Inside. Don't dawdle." The Reverend Frogmorton prodded her with a bony claw.

Abby stumbled through the low doorway into a dark passage. The Reverend Frogmorton laid a scratchy hand on her shoulder to guide her. She shivered.

They entered a gloomy room. There were several doorways and one small window. All were filled with heads pushing to see what would happen. No-one seemed to think it rude to be nosy.

Abby blinked a few times. What she had taken for a big grey shadow turned into the fattest man she had ever seen.

"Curtsey to your Lord Bishop," a cold voice ordered her out of the gloom.

6

The Fat Bishop

Abby stared hard at the fat Bishop. He was dressed in something which looked like a dressing gown with a fur collar. It had once been red but was now so dirty and stained with food which had been gobbled and spilled that it was the colour of mud. The inn-keeper was placing a metal plate piled with cakes in front of him.

Beside the Bishop stood a thin young man in black clothes which were turning green. He had a sneering nose, a pouty mouth and looked as if he was very pleased with himself but not with anyone else.

"Curtsey to your Lord Bishop," the thin young man repeated.

"Who are you?" Abby asked, deciding that with someone like that it was best from the very start to make it clear that she wasn't going to be bossed about.

"Don't be impertinent," he snapped. "I am Clerk to his Lordship. Do as I say."

"You don't curtsey when you're wearing jeans, you curtsey when you've got a skirt on," Abby pointed out. "You can have a bow instead," she said to the Bishop. She put an arm across her middle and leaned forward, the way she'd learned to do for a school play. "Is that all right?"

"Don't be insolent, child," the Clerk hissed, "or

the Lord Bishop will have you thrashed at every house in the village to teach you some manners."

The Bishop flicked his hand at the Clerk for silence.

"Child," the Bishop began in a squeaky voice which sounded as though the huge body was hiding a mouse, "I am told you are either a witch or mad. Which are you?"

"Think carefully before you answer," the Clerk put in, before she could speak. "If we suspect you to be a witch you will be thrown into the river with stones tied to you to see whether the Devil will save you."

"What if he does?" Abby asked, interested.

"Then we shall know you for a witch and you'll be burned at the stake." The Clerk gave a tight smile. "If we decide you are mad we shall beat you until we see the demons which possess you fly out of your mouth and nostrils and ears. So think before you answer."

Abby thought. This was worse than spelling tests at school. If she said she wasn't a witch they would drown her to prove it, and if she told them the truth, that she was lost in history, they would think she was mad.

She swallowed. She didn't seem to have much choice. She said the only thing she could think of which might get her out of the clutches of the Bishop and his Clerk.

"All right. I'm a witch," she announced.

"What?" the Bishop squeaked.

"I'm a witch."

"You can't be," the Clerk interrupted. "Witches never admit it. You must be mad."

Abby realised she hadn't thought of that answer to her brilliant idea. It was too late to change her mind now, so she just had to go on with it.

"You're very sure of yourself, Mr Clerk," Abby said, squinting at him threateningly. "Would you like to think again? While you're deciding, I'll just say a little spell. Abracadabra, ee-i-addy-o. Shall I go on?" Abby asked the Clerk. "Or can you already feel your stomach turning to frog's spawn? Abracadabra... "

"Stop!" the Clerk screamed, clutching his stomach. "She's a witch."

"Burn her," the Bishop squeaked.

"If anyone lays a hand on me," Abby warned them, "I'll make their blood boil, I'll turn their tongue into an adder and I'll squeeze snot out of every pore in their skin."

No-one moved.

What next? Abby wondered. How can I get out of here?

There was silence. Everyone else seemed to be thinking, "What next?" as well.

Then, from outside, came the sound of a panting voice crying wildly. One word was being repeated over and over again. As it drew nearer the voice became shriller.

In the inn everyone strained to hear what the voice was crying.

7

Abby and the Armada

The shouting voice came nearer.

"'Tis Alf," someone called out. "He be on watch."

Through the window they saw Alf, waving his arms and tearing across the sand dunes towards the village. His yellow hair was flapping in panic. Abby realised that this was the moment, after one of her sniffs, when she had seen Alf running towards her.

As he got nearer, his yells turned into words, "Spaniards!" he cried, panting. "Spaniards! There be a Spanish galleon coming into the bay."

"Haven't you defeated the Armada yet?" Abby asked.

"What's an Armada?" the Bishop squealed.

"Don't you know what the Armada is?" Abby asked in surprise. "Perhaps that's because it hasn't arrived yet. It's a huge Spanish fleet that came to invade England."

The Bishop gave a yelp.

"Her's a spy," Alf shouted through the window. Abby saw a hand come out of the crowd and clout him across the ear.

"Don't worry," Abby said encouragingly. "Sir Francis Drake will defeat it."

"Never heard of him," the Clerk snapped. "The girl's mad."

"We'll deal with her another time," the Bishop

piped, pleased to have found an excuse to get away from Abby. "My duty is clear. I shall ride poste-haste to town and alert the army." He turned to his Clerk. "Bring the rents."

"Light the beacon," the Clerk cried, sweeping up an armful of money bags from a table which was littered with empty plates as well as the one with cakes.

The Bishop grabbed a handful of cakes and waddled outside. The villagers were standing in an excited group.

"Good people," the Bishop squeaked. "It is your duty to delay the Spaniards for as long as you can." A cunning expression hid itself in the folds of his face. "We shall do the same, believe me." He raised a plump hand and blessed the crowd. "Fear not. The army will soon be here."

Six of the villagers heaved the Bishop onto his horse. Abby thought that it sagged in the middle but she couldn't be sure because once the Bishop was on it she couldn't see much of the poor animal.

The Bishop flapped his arms and legs and at last the horse began to stagger up the village street away from the sea and danger. The Clerk followed on his horse, breaking into a trot.

Then Abby remembered. They were the men on horses she'd seen when she'd sniffed. She remembered something else as well. There had been soldiers in armour.

"Hurray for the Lord Bishop," Alf shouted. Some of the villagers raised a feeble cheer, others looked doubtful.

"What are you going to do about that?" Abby asked, pointing at the tops of a row of masts which could just be seen above the sand dunes.

The villagers turned, then they all began to talk at once.

"Come on," Abby said to Wally, who was standing near her. "I want to see a real Spanish galleon."

They ran up to the top of the dunes to get a better view. A huge wooden ship with rows of cannons pointing at them was just lowering its anchor into the water. Its sails were tattered and one of the masts was broken.

"I remember," Abby said. "As well as Sir Francis Drake and his ships, there was a big storm which finished off the Armada."

"I expect they do come here to repair their mast and collect fresh water," Wally said.

The deck was crowded with men in helmets. As Abby watched, a boat was lowered into the water, then another and another.

Men in armour began climbing down ropes into them. Then a horse appeared on deck. It was blindfolded, tied in a sling and raised into the air by a system of pulleys which lowered it over the side towards one of the boats.

"I can't see the villagers of Withy Bottom stopping that lot for more than thirty seconds," Abby said.

"Oh, dearie me," a voice panted beside her. Abby looked round to find that Alf's nan had struggled up to the top of the dune. "Whatever shall us do?"

Other villagers were staring open-mouthed at the sight.

Abby spoke to them. "Good people of Withy Bottom," she cried. "You must follow the example of your Lord Bishop and get out of here fast."

They didn't need telling twice. Like a flock of birds they whirled round and fled after the Bishop, their rags flapping behind them.

But they didn't get far. Coming down the village street toward them was a strange white figure waving its arms.

"That be Master Ned the miller," Wally told Abby.

They hurried after the villagers. By the time they caught up, Master Ned had stopped panting enough to tell them his news.

"The withy beds be flooded," he cried.

"No they en't," Wally contradicted him. "We were there this morning."

"It were the Bishop," the miller shouted excitedly. "He opened the sluice-gate and let all the water out of the mill pond. He said it were to

delay the Spaniards. We're an island again."

The villagers suddenly understood. There was a groan from everyone at the same time.

"Now let me see if I've got this right," Abby said. "Does opening this sluice-gate mean we're trapped here?"

Wally nodded. "T'will take three hours for enough water to drain away so that we can cross to the mainland. By that time the Spaniards will have chopped us up small enough for lobster bait."

"Isn't there any other way to escape?"

"Only by boat," Wally said hopelessly, "and our boats be on the beach where the Spaniards are going to land."

Abby thought. "I've got an idea," she announced.

8

THE BATTLE OF WITHY BOTTOM

"What we've got to do is hold the Spaniards up long enough for the water to go down so that the villagers can escape to the mainland. Right?" Abby demanded.

"Right," Wally agreed. "Saying it's the easy bit."

"Will you help me?"

"I s'pose so." He didn't sound very enthusiastic.

"Good old Wally." Abby gave him an encouraging pat on the back which made him look even more worried. "Now, what I need are some rags and matches."

"What're matches?"

"Things to start a fire."

"I've got a tinder box." Wally frowned. "What're we going to do?"

"Set fire to the Spanish galleon, of course. I learned all about fire-ships at school," Abby said confidently. "You get a wind to blow a fire-ship into the enemy fleet, the ships all catch fire and sink."

Wally scratched his head. "Are you sure you bain't mad?" he asked. "We haven't got a fire-ship nor any gunpowder to pack it with."

"Cheer up Wally," Abby said excitedly. "We've got a raft and other things. Now let's go and fetch your tinder box and some rags. We'd better take an axe as well."

They collected all the items Abby wanted while the villagers ran around in circles like chickens with no heads, collecting their valuables before the Spaniards arrived. No-one noticed Abby and Wally scurrying off towards the place where the raft was hidden.

They arrived panting and pulled it out from its hiding-place under the willow tree.

"We must disguise it," Abby said. "Chop off some branches and fix them on so that it looks like an old tree floating down the river."

"I still doesn't see how we're going to set fire to a galleon," Wally said, doing as he was told. "It'll take more'n that bit of tinder to set her alight."

"You'll see in a minute." Abby grinned at her idea. "Cast off and paddle downstream to the Devil's Punch Bowl."

They steered the raft into the bank just below the pool of thick black oil.

"Come on." Abby laughed excitedly to encourage Wally and herself. "What we need first are Alf's wonky pots."

"You're going to fill them with this oil stuff," Wally exclaimed, his face suddenly brightening.

"Then we'll tie rags across the tops… "

"… and set fire to them like the lightning did." Wally stopped. "Then what?"

"We sail up to the galleon on our raft… "

"Boat."

"... boat, and throw them through the portholes."

Wally shook his head. "The gun-ports would be better. They're lower down, easier to reach."

They worked madly. When they had filled fourteen pots they ran out of rags and both were covered in oil.

"Come on," Abby cried. "Under the branches. We'll have to paddle lying down."

After putting the pots on the raft, they hid themselves and steered the raft out into the middle of the river. It drifted towards the galleon in the bay. A few minutes later the ship came into sight.

"I can see Spanish soldiers on the beach," Wally whispered. "There be four horses as well."

"Steer for the side of the ship away from the beach," Abby hissed back.

They drifted silently up to the galleon and bumped against its side like a log carried by the current. Abby peered up through the tangle of leaves which hid her. The ship looked as though it was going to roll over on top of them. She swallowed nervously. They couldn't possibly set fire to it. The wood was wet and the planks were as thick as trees.

"I can't see anyone on this side," she muttered to Wally, trying to sound confident.

"I expect they be all too busy unloading on the beach side."

"It sounds like it," Abby agreed. "They're making enough noise."

"So much the better for us," Wally said.

"You'll have to work the tinder-box," Abby decided. "I don't know how to. I'll climb up onto that ledge." She pointed to a thick beam which jutted out just below a row of square holes that ran the length of the ship. Those must be the gun-ports, she thought.

"All right," Wally said, sounding relieved. "I'll light the rags and pass the pots up to you."

Abby pushed the branches aside and stood up. When a wave lifted the raft she made a grab for the nearest hole. Inside it she saw the black, pitted barrel of a cannon. The raft bobbed down again, leaving her hanging there. She swung one leg up onto the ledge, then the other and wriggled herself into a crouching position.

She stretched out a hand for the first fire-bomb.

"Give me a bomb quick," she hissed. The waves below seemed to be trying to reach up to pluck her off the slippery ledge. She tried not to look down.

Wally had a little flame going in his tinder-box. He blew on it and dipped the end of some rags in it. For a few seconds nothing happened, then the oil-soaked rag flared up and started to burn like a candle wick. He passed the first of the bombs up to Abby.

She dropped it through the gun-port. There was a crash as the pot broke. They looked at each other, not able to move, while they waited to hear a shout from inside the ship. Nothing happened.

"They be making too much noise," Wally whispered.

Abby nodded, hardly daring to breathe. "It hasn't worked."

"Try another."

The raft was rubbing gently against the side of the galleon and drifting slowly with the current. Abby dug her fingers into the wood and slipped along to the next gun-port, pressing herself flat against the sides of the ship.

Wally had another bomb alight. They became quicker. The raft drifted. Abby scrambled. Wally lit. The bomb went thought the gun-port.

But nothing happened. There were no flames to delay the Spaniards and save the village.

They posted twelve bombs into the ship, but then the current suddenly took the raft and plucked it away from the shelter of the hull.

Wally grabbed a paddle and tried to force it back.

"The current's too strong," he called hoarsely. "Quick, jump. You'll have to swim. I s'pose you can swim?" he asked, as an afterthought.

Abby let go and dropped into the water gasping at the cold. Her mouth closed automatically, but she made her eyes stay open. She kicked hard and began to swim towards the raft. The current was pushing her along as well as the raft. She knew she could catch it easily. She had done her personal survival badge and swum in her clothes. Anyway, I needed a bath, she thought, as she kicked herself forward.

Wally paddled to steady the raft. Abby got nearer. As she stretched out a hand to grab it, there was a shout from the ship behind her.

"They've seen us," Wally cried, catching hold of her arm.

She struggled onto the raft. There was a sudden bang from the ship.

"They be shooting at us!" Wally shouted. "Paddle for your life."

They knelt and dipped their paddles. The current had already carried them some way from the ship.

"We must get away before they reload," Wally panted.

Within half a minute they were well clear of the ship. There had been only one shot.

They looked back. The ship appeared just as it had before they'd attacked it.

"What's happened to our bombs?" Abby moaned in despair.

9

The End of the Witch of Withy Bottom

The current swept Abby and Wally across the bay. They sat amongst the willow branches and let the raft drift.

Abby shivered. "We've failed."

"Well, us tried our best," Wally said reassuringly.

Suddenly he leapt to his feet. "Look there!" he shouted.

Black smoke was beginning to trickle out of one of the gun-ports.

"It's working," Abby whispered. "Come on. More, more, more!"

Obediently, smoke began to belch out of other gun-ports.

"Are you sure you bain't a witch?" Wally asked, laughing.

"I wish I was," Abby said. "I'd give some of the people I've met here stomachache, I can tell you."

Wally jigged about and made the raft rock. "The ship's on fire, the ship's on fire, the ship's on fire," he chanted.

"Let's paddle for the shore," Abby said. "No-one will be bothered about us now."

They bumped ashore behind some rocks, a little way past the beach where the Spaniards had been landing, and pulled the raft clear of the waves.

"Let's us see what's happening," Wally

whispered.

They climbed over the rocks until they were able to see the beach and the galleon.

"Look at that!" Abby gasped in amazement at what they had done.

The huge ship was half hidden by billowing smoke. Occasionally flames could be seen cutting through the black clouds and leaping like lizards' tongues after their prey. Ropes, sails and wood were all food for the monster which Abby and Wally had released from the tinder-box.

"We slowed them down all right," Wally murmured.

They turned to look at the beach. Only one Spaniard stood there holding the reins of the four horses and looking uneasily over his shoulder. The rest of the soldiers were in boats heading back to the ship as fast as they could to fight the fire.

Abby and Wally stood up. From the top of the rocks they could see the village. Some of the villagers were standing in the street looking back at the column of smoke.

Abby began to jump up and down. "Come back! There's only one soldier left. Come back!"

At that moment there was a tremendous *Boom.*

Their ears popped. The deck of the Spanish galleon rose into the air and planks showered into the sea.

"Gunpowder," Wally whispered. "The fire

must've made the gunpowder explode."

Suddenly the rope holding the anchor snaked into the water, its end burned through. The ship began to drift out to sea. There were cries from the soldiers in the boats and their oars went faster as they chased after it.

"Come on," Abby said pulling Wally after her, "we must get down to the beach and make the Spaniard with the horses our prisoner."

"Are you sure this be a good idea?" Wally asked, as he stumbled after her.

The soldier was standing open-mouthed as he watched his ship drift away and the soldiers from the rowing boats scramble on board to put out the fire.

Abby marched up to him.

"Good afternoon," she said politely, and bowed. "I'm afraid your ship's gone without you, so you can't get away. Do you understand?" The Spaniard and the horses stared at them. "You are our prisoner. Please give us your sword." She pointed at it.

The soldier seemed to understand and obediently pulled his sword from his belt and handed it hilt first to Abby.

He gave a little bow. "Señor Angel," he said with a strange accent. He had black hair and dark eyes.

"What did he say?" Wally asked.

"He said 'Señor Angel'," Abby answered.

"That's his name in Spanish. In English he'd be Mr Angel."

As she said it, her eyes opened wide in amazement. It had to be. It must be. Señor Angel was the foreign sailor her nan had told her about. The one her family...

"Wally, do you know who this is?" Abby gasped.

"He said he were Señor Angel," Wally said puzzled.

"I think he's my great-great-great-great-great-great-great-great-great-great-great-great-grandfather!"

"In that case, we'd better look after him very carefully," Wally said, not seeming surprised about anything where Abby was concerned.

"He's got to stay in Withy Bottom – or I'll never be born!" Abby exclaimed.

"I've got an idea what you could say," Wally whispered.

Villagers started to arrive on the beach. Señor Angel went on holding the horses and looking as if he couldn't think what else to do. When everyone seemed to be there, Abby made the announcement that Wally has suggested.

"Good people of Withy Bottom," Abby said, waving her sword boldly. "Wally and I have saved you from the Spaniards. This gentleman holding the horses is Señor Angel. Now listen carefully.

The Parish of Withy Bottom will have good luck so long as he lives here and is well treated. Never forget that."

There was a cheer for Abby and Wally and the innkeeper brought out a barrel of beer and the cakes which the fat Bishop had left behind. A beach party started and Abby was pleased to see that Alf looked fed up and rather left out.

Later in the afternoon, when the party was in full swing, someone started shouting, "The Duke! The Duke!" and a few minutes later a man on a horse followed by a long line of men armed with pikes, swords and pitchforks marched onto the sand.

The Duke reined in his horse and gazed out to sea where the Spanish galleon was now only a small, smoky dot on the horizon.

Abby took a good look at him at the same time. He wore a floppy hat with a feather – rather like Nan's – armour on his top half only and a crinkly concertina collar which had lost its starch and drooped. Abby wondered how the English had managed to defeat the Armada. They seemed a pretty sloppy lot.

"Who's in charge here?" the Duke asked at last.

None of the villagers seemed to want to speak.

Abby stepped forward. "I suppose I am," she said. "My name's Abigail Angel. Is that the army?" She pointed at the untidy line of men behind him.

The Duke leaned back and laughed. "Well may you ask, young lady. This was the best army I could find today."

"In that case," Abby said, "it's a good job we defeated the Spaniards before you arrived." She sneezed. "I seem to be getting a cold. I got wet after we set fire to the ship."

"I like your spirit, Abby," the Duke told her, "and I begin to see how a few villagers could defeat a ship loaded with the finest army in the world."

"I'm not a villager, at least, not properly," Abby corrected him. "But never mind that. I should like to ask you a favour."

"You deserve a reward, so ask."

"It's not a reward," Abby said seriously. "It's a swop. You see, Wally and I captured these horses," she pointed to the horses, "and what I should like you to do is swop them for some oxen so that the people of Withy Bottom can plough the land properly again. What do you say, Duke?"

"They're fine animals. I shall do it gladly." He jumped down from his horse. "Now tell me how you fired the galleon."

"It were witchcraft," Alf's voice suddenly shouted out, "begging your honour's pardon."

"Who are you, fellow?" the Duke demanded.

"He's the village idiot," Abby put in.

"I'm Alf, the apprentice potter, your Lordship," Alf said. "I was hiding in the dunes, waiting for a chance to attack the Spaniards, when I saw her do her magic. Her stood on yonder rocks and danced and shouted a spell, and all the fiery demons in the air rushed down onto the ship and blew it up. I seed it with my own eyes, your Lordship."

"What do you say to that, Abby?" the Duke asked, with a smile.

But before she had time to answer, there came the sound of a squeaky voice crying, "Make way. Stand aside," and the fat Bishop rode into view followed by his Clerk.

"Ah," the Bishop piped, "I see you have caught the witch child."

"Her's no witch," Wally suddenly burst out. "I'll tell you what we did, and it was no more witchery than what a cannon is."

There was a babble of voices.

"Silence!" the Duke thundered. "You, boy," he pointed at Wally. "You shall tell your story."

"Thank you, my Lord. I shall tell you truly." Wally scratched his head. "When the Spaniards came, the Lord Bishop fled and as he went he opened the sluice-gate and trapped us here."

There was a murmur of support from the villagers. The Bishop looked as though he were trying to shrink.

"Then Abby and me went to my boat. On it we piled pots of the black oil from the Devil's Punch

Bowl. The pots be those misshapen ones Alf said he'd sold, but they be hidden by the river bank."

Several puzzled faces turned towards Alf and it was his turn to look as though he were trying to shrink.

"We tied rags round the pots," Wally went on, "floated to the Spanish ship, lit them and dropped them through the gun-ports. T'was no witchery, I swear."

"Give me an army of children like these," the Duke declared, "and I will conquer the world for Her Majesty. If this is witchcraft, then anyone who wins a battle is a witch."

"It is the Church who must decide who is a witch and who not," a grating voice announced. The Bishop's Clerk bustled forward. "I have felt her power," he said, waving a finger at Abby. "Only this noontide she tried to turn my stomach to frog's spawn."

"More likely," the Duke answered, "you ate too much fruit for breakfast."

"My Lord may mock me," the Clerk said, smiling humourlessly, "but smelling out witches is my task, not the Duke's."

"Her's no witch," Nan said, stepping forward. "Her's a little angel as saved us all."

"Quiet, woman," the Clerk snapped. "See this, girl?" he sneered, waving something under Abby's nose so close that she couldn't see it. "Garlic. Your spells cannot harm me now. What do you say to that?"

"I had some garlic bread once," Abby told him. "It was quite nicc, but everyone said my breath smelt horrible after it. So I shouldn't eat too much if I were you."

The Duke laughed. "She's a match for you any day, Master Clerk."

"A match for me, is she? I shall test her and you will see."

Suddenly, he pulled a leather pouch from his belt. "This will drive the demons out of her." He plunged his hand in the pouch and flung a handful of dust into her face.

"Pepper!" a voice cried, but Abby could not see who.

"Atishoo!" She sneezed. The she sneezed again, and again, and again.

It was as though she was blowing out all the sniffs she had ever taken. She thought she would never stop.

As she sneezed, pictures whirled through her head. Everything that had ever happened in Withy Bottom or Woodford Green passed before her eyes.

Then the sneezing stopped. She seemed to be floating in a dark bed which was so soft she could not feel it.

In the distance she heard voices – Alf's nan saying, "What have you done with our angel, Master Clerk?"

The Duke asking, "Do witches usually disappear when you throw pepper in their faces?"

Wally crying, "Her was no witch – her was an angel from heaven."

The Bishop greedily squeaking, "I declare that Abby was an angel. We shall build a church and a shrine. Pilgrims will flock here and give money to support them."

The innkeeper announcing, "Pilgrims can rest at the inn and us'll call it The Angel Inn. Señor Angel can work for me."

Last of all she heard Wally saying, "Her did say that the true name of Withy Bottom were Woodford Green. Let us change the name in her honour."

Then Abby opened her eyes and saw a car.

10

The Mystery of Woodford Green

Abby took a deep breath and yelled.

"What's that horrible stink up my nose?"

"It's smelling salts," her own nan's voice said, "and don't say stink, it's not nice."

"I thought it was pepper."

Abby found that she was lying on the pavement in Woodford Green.

"What am I doing down here?"

"You fainted," Nan told her in her tut-tut voice. "Too much stale school air, I expect. We must get you home."

With that, Nan walked into the middle of the road, held up her hand, stopped the first taxi that came and ordered them both a lift home.

Abby lay on the settee and thought about Withy Bottom while she waited for the doctor.
He arrived at last, asking, "Now what seems to be the trouble?"

"I was just walking along behind Nan," Abby explained, "breathing deeply, when I suddenly couldn't stop. I breathed in and in until I felt I was going to explode, and I saw all these pictures of things in the past, then I wasn't here any more."

The doctor frowned. "Has she had an attack like this before?" he asked Nan.

"She's told me some nonsense about smelling pictures," Nan agreed. "But that was just to try to get out of our daily walk. I always insist," Nan went on before the doctor could interrupt, "that she take plenty of deep breaths to get the stale school air out of her lungs. How many children that air has been in and out of, collecting germs, I can't imagine, but," Nan rushed on like a walking race, "I make a point of taking Abby for a walk each afternoon to clear her lungs."

Nan stopped.

The doctor frowned again. "I see. I see," he muttered. He lifted Abby's eyelids and squinted through a torch. He listened to her chest and hit her with a rubber hammer.

Then he said, "Aah, umm, er, yes, I see." He turned back to Nan. "Deep breathing, did you say?"

Nan said so again.

"Hyperventilation," the doctor said at last.

"What?" Abby exclaimed in alarm.

"No more deep breathing," the doctor ordered.

"No more walks?" Abby asked eagerly.

"Ah now… " the doctor began to say.

"All right," Abby said, before he could finish. "I'll just sit quietly and watch television."

"What?" Nan exploded.

"Nothing to worry about." The doctor patted Abby's hand. "Take it easy for a while."

"Humph!" Nan snapped her lips together.

Abby smiled sweetly at the doctor. "Do you know how Woodford Green got its name, by any chance?"

"You're interested in local history, are you?" the doctor chuckled. "Local history is my hobby, too. Did you know?"

"That's a bit of luck," Abby said.

"There's a mystery," the doctor told her, "about the name of our town. It's old name was Withy Bottom. Then quite suddenly everyone started calling it Woodford Green. There's no record of any ford across the river here. So what do you make of that?"

"Something important must have happened," Abby suggested, "and people changed the name in honour of it."

"Good idea," the doctor agreed, getting ready to leave. "Now all you have to do is find out what that was."

I already know that, Abby thought.

She couldn't wait for the next day so that she could tell Walid what had happened to her. But she wouldn't tell Mr Alfreds. He'd only make fun of her and start calling her Señorita Angel or something else Spanish.

Abby frowned. Now that she thought about it, the people in the past had been a bit like the people she knew in her own time. Wally had been her friend just like Walid. And Alf had been their enemy like Mr Alfreds. And Nan had been there when she needed her like her Nan. Perhaps

everyone else had been like people she knew. She'd have to think about it.

Nan came back from showing the doctor out.

"You know the shipwrecked sailor called Mr Angel who we're named after?" Abby asked. "Well, he wasn't a shipwrecked sailor, he was a left-behind soldier, and his name was Señor Angel. Can I have the television on, please?"

"Watching television is probably what's wrong with you," Nan said unsympathetically. "Haven't you got any homework to do?"

"No. We're doing the Spanish Armada at school and I know all about that." Abby made herself more comfortable on the settee. "There's a good programme on about now."

Nan said, "Tut-tut," but put the television on.

Abby sniffed. "I think I'm getting a cold."

"Blow your nose. Don't sniff."

"It's all right," Abby promised her. "My nose is all blocked up. I can't smell a thing."

She sniffed to prove it.